So, This Actually Happened: Tales from a reTIRED Teacher

TRACI D. W. JACKSON

Contents

Dedication

This book is dedicated to my mother who always encouraged me to be a teacher that makes a difference; and to my father who always encouraged me to embrace the joy in moving on. "Two tears in a bucket, fuck it!"

Introduction

When I decided to retire after ten years into my career, I realized that adulthood was real...real bullshit. I often think back to the young, bright-eyed, bushy-tailed unstoppable teacher I was when I began in 2007. The classroom inspired me. My students inspired me. The questions inspired me. Everything inspired me to educate. Have you seen those t-shirts with the slogan "I'm a teacher, what's your SUPERPOWER?" I am pretty sure that I inspired that t-shirt. I didn't need a red cape; I had colored paper, a hot glue gun and comfortable flats. There was nothing that I couldn't create with colored paper and a hot glue gun. My glue-gun construction skills were so tight. If I needed it for a lesson or if my students needed it as a tool for learning, I was going to make it. Teaching was my first SUPERPOWER and glue-gun amazement was my second. But back to teaching, my classroom was always bright and student-centered. I would fly down the halls in a flash, with the intention of not wasting one single minute. I was challenged to instruct from the first bell to the last bell, and damn it that was exactly what I was going to do. Who needs lunch, not me! Why? because I was a SUPERTEACHER. Fuck that, I was an Ignorance Officer. My mission was to open minds and hearts through exposure and love, one lesson at a time. I was placed in the classroom to arm my students with the love and guidance it takes to positively change the world. At the very least I knew I could single-handedly change an entire community or two. I was ready everyday to Michelle Pfeiffer in *Dangerous Minds* that shit. No, I've never been a Marine and I didn't know any sick-ass karate moves but I did have candy; and lots of it. I was ready! I was an Ignorance Officer, professionally dressed in sensible flats and a holster of candy, sharpened pencils and tissues. (Tissues are a must; you'd be amazed by the frequency kids need to blow their noses.) Whelp, that was me ten years ago.

Today, I look at the fat lady in the wrinkled shirt, old gym shoes and one long gray hair named after the student I'm certain was the cause of it, and I ask, "what the hell just happened?"

I think a few things happened. One, a constant practice of delusional depictions of specific events; two, continuous and excessive deflection from blatant reality; three, persistent experimenting with alternative truths. See, I'm still doing it. After ten years it's become a habit. I'll just come right out and say it.... THE LIES, all the lies, the little white lies, the bold black lies, the yellow I'm-telling-you-this-to-spare-your-feelings-lies and the red angry I'm-telling-you-this-to-hurt-your-feelings-lies. It doesn't matter the color or the cause they are all lies, and I'm tired of them. It's time for a little truth around here.

The truth is, there is too much red tape in education today. Teachers have their hands tied! We can't tell students the truth because they'll tell their parents and parents will report us to have us fired. Teachers can't speak freely to parents because they will be offended, and then report us to have us fired. Teachers can't complain to administration because they'll report that we aren't fit for the job and have us fired. So, who speaks up? NO ONE! Why? Because, you can't afford to be fired when you have more than a few bills and mounds of outstanding student loan debt. BUT, if you retire, you can talk all you want. So I'm talking. Here it goes.

CHAPTER 1

Tired of Hearing About Cursive

So, this actually happened. 2016 was the year of "yo hairline." What is "yo hairline" you ask? Great question! "Yo hairline" is the idiotic reincarnation of the "Deez Nuts" joke. Remember back in the day when a classmate would ask you a question like, "What's in your mouth?" And before you could answer, a grape *Now and Later*, they would scream, "DEEZ NUTS!" and everyone would laugh. Or you might be on an elevator and a friend would say, "press that" and you'd ask "press what"? and they'd yell, "DEEZ NUTS." You get the gist, right? Well, "yo hairline" works the same way.

By August 2016, the joke finally trickled all the way down to elementary schools, and by October 2016, the students in the prekindergarten class at my school got ahold of the phrase. Now, if you have ever seen a prekindergarten class, you know that it should be against the law to have that much cute in one place, at one time. They are so small and adorable. At my school there was one little cutie in particular who stole everyone's heart. He would be the runt of the litter, if he was a pup; so tiny and cute. He could have easily been in a GAP kids ad. I would talk to him every-day after school. He was kinda shy at first. Just making faces from across the room. One day, he spotted me with my tablet after school. He finally came over, and spoke. "What's that?" he said in a high-pitched mousy voice. I replied, "a tablet, you know what this is." Then, he asked to play a game and I let him. After that, he came to visit me everyday during dismissal. This went on for a few months. Then around November, I'd figured we were close enough and had been in school long enough to have a real conversation. So when he came to visit me I said, "Hey, what did you learn today?" He answered "Yo hairline." WHAT?! "That's not cute or funny, what did you learn today?" I demanded. "Yo hairline," he insisted. Then I challenged him, "boy, you can say all that but can you spell your name?" "No", he said. (His name was four letters long.) I told him, "You can't go to kindergarten saying stuff like that and not being able to spell your name!" He said, "Who is kindergarten? I don't know no kindergarten." No you don't young man, no you don't. That day my favorite little prekindergarten student instantly became way less cute.

Now, answer me this, why does a four and a half year old, who spends more than eight hours a day away from home not know how to spell his own name? I didn't ask him to spell his mama name. I didn't ask him to spell my name. I simply asked him to spell his very own, four-letter, first name; and he couldn't. That's a damn shame. But whose damn shame is it? You better not say his teachers! That's the problem. Teachers can't do everything, and parents, you can't wait for teachers to do it all. If you wait until your child starts school, waiting on the teacher to teach him his name and how to spell it, you are setting your child up for failure; a complete disaster. And, that's a damn shame. At some point, village, you must realize that this is your child too and if the mama and daddy suck, somebody has to step in and teach the child survival skills. Reading is a survival skill. Basic math is a survival skill. Knowing how to get home, or at least your address is a survival skill. Knowing how to clean yo ass is a survival skill. Knowing how to tell time is a survival skill. Knowing how to count money and give change is a survival skill. Knowing how to follow directions is a survival skill. And, knowing how to spell your four letter, first name is a motherfuckin' survival skill.

Teachers don't teach survival skills, teachers expand upon survival skills. If your child knows their address, their teacher will teach them the difference in a city and a state. If your child knows the letters of the alphabet, their teacher will teach them how to combine letters to form words. If your child knows their numbers, teachers show them how to make more or less, or to divide numbers among friends. The parent is the child's very first teacher. The parent is the child's very first teacher. (That wasn't a typo.) The classroom teacher is there to grow and support

> The parent is the child's very first teacher.

the child. Parents, you have to give teachers something to work with besides a well-dressed, cute face. At least teach your child some damn survival skills.

I had a student who was adopted by his mother's husband on a random day, smack-dap in the middle of a random month. The mother didn't tell any teacher directly that her son's name had been changed. She simply went to registrar and submitted the paperwork and boom, the student's name was changed in the system. So, when I went to add grades for my student, he no longer existed. Befuddled, (yes, I curse and say words like befuddled) I told him that he was missing. He then informed me that his name was legally changed. I asked my 4th grade, almost eleven-year-old student to spell his last name and… you already know he couldn't. Now, even more perplexed, I asked him his new name, expecting him to say Zagerbifendorf, Sookramor, or Uhl. This kid says Cooper. REALLY?! The parents only had to teach him five letters, since you use one on them twice, and didn't. He thought the shit started with a K. And, that's the teacher fault?! Hell, no it's not. Place all that blame on the sorry ass parents and the sorry ass village to match. Who saved the day and taught him how to spell his new name before he left school that day. This teacher, who had other kids whose names weren't stolen from them at night. This teacher who had a bomb-ass lesson plan to teach. This teacher who wanted to eat during her lunch instead of teaching remedial naming 101.

As I listen to parents complain at PTA, in friend conversations and random places like the bank, I often here the question "Why are they not teaching cursive?" "What happened to cursive?" Cursive?! Fucking cursive?! Teachers want to teach cursive. But we can't, cause on the first day of school, you keep dropping off empty mannequins called kids who don't know the number of the school bus they just got off, or how to spell their own first name and you expect us to work a miracle with no support from you or the village in 180 days. NOT. GON. HAPPEN.

> Teachers want to teach cursive.

What teachers' want is for you to prepare your children for education. Teachers spend their summers getting ready to hit the ground running on the first day of school. Instead, they are left still lacing up running shoes after the gun sounds. And yes, some kids will catch up in the race. Some students may even win.

But, generally it's only one kid and it's not yours. Lace up parents, lace up village, cause us teachers are tired of being left behind and running a losing race.

CHAPTER 2

Tired of Teaching Ugly Kids

So, this actually happened. I had a parent who was extremely difficult to contact. The phone numbers were always disconnected. Her children never memorized the updated number. She would never send a note with her current number. She rarely came up to the school to check on her children and notes home...who knows what happened to those. Luckily, we did have an unofficial emergency number that was passed down with her children each year. It was the number of the paternal grandmother. The student's mother and father were no longer a couple due to what appeared to be a bad break-up, and the tension was more than obvious. Using this number was a only Break Glass in Case of Emergency number. You knew that when you used it, you were possibly opening the door to some

Jerry Springer type shit. As a professional we have to exhaust all resources when attempting to contact the parent for meetings. So, that means using the dirty, no-good, left behind, consistently reliable relatives number. I called Granny…and she answered. Granny told me that she would contact mom and if should couldn't reach her she'd be glad to fill in for her at the meeting. She stated that she missed the children and wanted to see them anyway. The next day, what did I get?! A handwritten note from mom that read, "call me" with the updated number. I figured I needed to call quickly, mainly because I didn't know how long I had before it would be out of service. Even a powerful Ignorance Officer like myself is no match to the magical vanishing phone number. It's like a digit disappears every half-hour. When it vanishes, it's gone forever. So, time was precious when it came to this number. I had to call immediately. I figured since the students just got to school, she had to be awake. I was wrong. When she answered after a few rings, I could tell that my call had messed up some really good sleep. Mom quickly agreed on a date and time to meet. I hung up excited because she didn't curse me out.

The day of the meeting I had a 50/50 chance that she would show up. Why do people say that? Isn't everything you attempt to do in life a 50/50 chance? It kinda goes without needing to be said, right? Luck was in my favor because she showed up. We had our meeting, paperwork was updated, a new temporary phone number was provided and the meeting was adjourned. Except, mom didn't leave. She remained seated. You could tell she was deep in thought, so I remained seated too. She began to talk, and talk, and talk. She said, "I don't like kids." I had to remind her that she has four. The mother continued, "I know. Kids are too loud. I make them live down the street at my mother's house. They come to my house after school to do their homework but when they finish or get too noisy they have to go to my moms. They get on the bus for school from her house. Kids just do too much." I thought to myself, "and it took your dumb ass three more kids to figure this out!" What I decided to say was, "Yes, multiple kids can be a handful." What I also thought was "Don't have no more kids!"

She was lucky. She had two children at our school. Her eldest child was sweet, tried hard and generally wanted to do better. He wasn't that bright, but he was determined. Her other son was a shit-starter. He was always into some mess, but he was smart. The boys were loved by some teachers, liked by most and tolerated by all of their teachers. Loving students is a choice. Teachers are obligated to teach students to the best of our ability. That's the job. Anything else we do is for

> Loving students is a choice.

the love of the craft and the little person. If you have a teacher that loves your child, appreciate them because the love is genuine, pure and kind. Don't try to take advantage of their love because it sours the relationship. If you know the field trip cost seven dollars, don't send five dollars and note, just because you don't want to be inconvenienced with

> Don't try to take advantage of their love.

finding two more dollars. When a teacher loves a child, that student will be showered with love daily. You shouldn't do anything to make the teacher think they must hold back. Withholding love really stunts your child's growth and the teacher's joy.

That mom would take advantage of my nice teacher demeanor quite often. I never made her sweet child go without though. The bad one, he would go without all the time, especially once he fell too far behind to catch up with his classwork. What I have noticed over the years is NO one likes dumb, badass, ugly kids. You can always find one person to encourage a dumb kid. You can always find someone to guide a bad kid. You can always find a person that will love an ugly kid. But when a kid is dumb and bad as hell, it makes them ugly. They are hard to love. And generally, their own parents don't even like them. That's why they are NEVER absent from school. You have to choose. You can be dumb, that's ok. Every clique has a one designated smarty and a designated dummy. Everyone is dumb to somebody. You can be bad. It's understandable to have less than stellar behavior at times. Maybe you're going through something. Maybe you haven't been taught better. The problem occurs with the word AND. Bad and dumb isn't an option. You should have to choose. It's just bad parenting to let them be both.

Now the ugly word I know offended you, and that's ok. I understand. Although attractiveness applies, I am

> Bad and dumb isn't an option.

not referring to physical appearance but more of attitude. Dumb and bad yields a completely undesirable child. Completely undesirable is just a softer phrase for ugly.

Another reason nobody likes the dumb, badass, ugly child is because they require too much attention. You can't let them work in a group with other students because they function at a much lower rate than the rest of the group, and that leads to playing and disruptive behaviors to cover up that fact that they don't know shit. You can't let them work alone because they are bad as hell and cannot be trusted; eyeing your damn cell phone all day. Lastly, other kids don't want to work with them because of their ugly, fucked up attitude. So, that leaves the only adult in a room, aka the teacher, to spend even more time with the misfit crew, while the scholars are not being challenged.

What teachers' want are for you, parents, to realize that we have no special powers. If you know your child is more than challenging, don't send them to school when they're sleepy or sick. We want you to minimize our time with them. No, they can't stay for before-school clubs or after-school tutorial. The mandatory eight-ish hours are more than enough. Lastly, we want parents to speak up. The squeaky wheel gets the oil. In the classroom the squeaky wheel is generally the dumb, badass child. So the other kids suffer. Until teachers become leaders in education, we need parents to understand that their voices reign supreme. No one cares what the loud, dumb ass parent of the dumb, badass child has to say but when the loud, demanding parent of the sweet, scholarly child speaks up, people move.

CHAPTER 3

Tired of Peter Pan Syndrome

So, this actually happened. I was teaching in a middle school. It was the beginning of the academic year. The sixth graders were excited, hustling through the halls, overly confused. Out the corner of my eye I noticed a white-haired granny. She seemed to know many of the sixth grade students but was following two students in particular. As the day went on, I witnessed all of the students become more familiar with their new surroundings, helping friends to classes they had earlier in the day. Then, out the corner of my eye I saw the white-haired granny again. I thought it was odd that she was still around but I had too much to do to waste time inquiring about her. A few hours later the dismissal bell rang. Kids flooded the hall...and so did granny. She told the two brothers whom she'd been following, which bus to ride and that she'd pick them up from the bus stop in a few minutes. Then, she told the sixth grade teachers that she would see them tomorrow. Tomorrow, huh? So, as you can imagine granny was a topic of conversation during our end-of-first-day staff meeting. One of the sixth grade teachers asked, "What are we going to do about granny? When she was in my class, she explained that she has joined her grandsons' in every class, everyday since they started first grade. She aides them with their classwork, homework and remembering their belongings at the end of the day. There is nothing wrong with the boys. She just thinks she's supporting them. Apparently, she completed elementary school with them." Then, the teacher looked directly at the principal and slowly said, "She plans to join them everyday in class throughout middle school as well." I know you don't believe me. I didn't believe my ears when I heard it either. But, the next morning when I saw granny sitting at a desk in the back of math class, I knew there must have been some truth to this absurdity.

Every teacher's favorite assignment is the one written in the parent's penmanship that the child cannot explain. It makes us laugh, big belly laughs; deep down from within belly laughs. Go to the classroom teacher next door, shouting "hey look at

We work with your child all day, everyday.

this" belly laughs. And, we are laughing at you, parents. We work with your child all day, everyday; we know what their work looks like. If you do everything for your child, when will they learn to do it for themselves? You can't smother them and make it their teacher's issue. Teachers have a due date on homework for a reason. No, your child can't have an extension; our grades are due. Teachers hand out assignments on a set day for a reason. No, your child can't have extra credit; they didn't complete the actual credit. Teachers are in the business of building functional future citizens of the world, not coddling your immature, entitled, self-absorbed little snot of a kid.

It is not the teacher's job to cater to your child. If I hear, "but" from a parent one more time, I am going to scream. If I tell you that Joey hasn't turned in homework in a month and he has a zero, the last thing I want the parent to say is "BUT

> It is not the teacher's job to cater to your child.

he said he didn't have any homework." Teacher's want to use the but word too. As in, BUT that's not our problem, or BUT that little clown is a liar, or BUT he's still failing. Parents stop trying to make it our problem, it's not. Teachers have a deadline and goals to reach and you making lame-ass excuses for your child doesn't help us reach them.

I once had a student steal from me. I called his mother who immediately came to the school. We confronted her child together about the stolen property. The student denied theft to our faces, looking his mother in the eye and telling a bold-faced lie. Then, after we questioned him and talked faster than he could think, he admitted to stealing and gave a weak-ass apology. The mother then looked at me and said, "He misses his father, they don't have a relationship." Is that a good excuse for taking MY shit?! Hell, I don't have a relationship with his father either but you don't see me stealing. I'm not saying that the absence of his father isn't a deeply rooted issue that he may deal with daily. What I am saying is that his father's absence isn't the reason he stole my shit. He stole my shit because he wanted it.

What teachers' want is for you parents, to not condone the bullshit. This is your child to teach, not handicap. Stop doing everything for them and making excuses for them. And definitely, stop getting upset with us and reporting us when we refuse to handicap them the way you are. Guide them and teach them the way. Most importantly, give us the freedom to guide them toward long-term independence in our own way.

CHAPTER 4

Tired of ADHD
(All Day Hella Drama!)

So, this actually happened. The time was 7:30am. I was in my classroom trying to get things situated for the day, when my door flies open. My second grade student walks in speaking loudly, He says "HEY! I just came to tell you that I didn't take my medicine today, so I plan on being bad and getting on your nerves. You know I can't sit still and I have anger issues." I answered with the only response I could think of for a disrespectful child that early in the morning. "Who are you talking to? Walk back out that door and let's try this again the right way." The student walked out, turned around, knocked on the door, then asked to come inside. We greeted one another with pleasantries, and then he spoke in a tone appropriate for a

conversation and confessed to not taking his medication that morning. I explained to him that it was
ok. I inquired about why he felt the absence of medicine would allow him the privilege of being unruly
and getting on my nerves without consequence. My
student stated, quite matter-of-factly, "My medicine
helps me do my work and be nice, if I don't take it I
just can't control myself." He was obviously repeating
words that had been ingrained in his young mind by
an adult with few expectations for him. Don't nobody
got time for ADD; all-day drama.

We must be conscious of the information we tell
our children; basically because they're listening. Even
though they don't act like it, they hear you, are inter-
nalizing your words and will repeat it. I have heard
adults say things like, "You need this medicine to sit
down." "Your teacher said you were fighting, yelling
and cursing. You didn't take your pill today, did you?"
Then there is my favorite, "You know how you are
when you don't take your vitamin." What does any
of that shit mean? After you've heard any of these
excuses for long enough, the message begins to change.
"You need this medicine to sit down" translates to:
you are only expected to be conduct yourself properly
when you are on your medication. "Your teacher said
you were fighting, yelling and cursing. You didn't take
your pill today, did you?" translates to: its ok to act
like a damn fool when you're not on your medication,
I expect it…and your teacher does too. And then we

have, "You know how you act when you don't take your vitamin." This answers the question for the child before it's even asked. This statement translates to: please act like a complete fool! Act like you were born with the genes of Busta Rhymes and Lil' Jon. Act like your name was changed to Awfda Hooks and for 24 hours you have the right to embody the epitome of every international feel good song; *Hey Ya!* I'm so *Happy*, I plan to *Push It* to the limit. I probably Won't *Stop Til You Get Enough*. Hell, I just might go *All Night Long*. And while they are feeling good, teachers, peers, and strangers are all watching the shit-show.

Expectations are a strong belief something will happen. What are your strong beliefs for your kids? Do you believe he will go to college, except when he doesn't take his medicine? Do you believe she will become a prima ballerina...except when she doesn't take her medicine? Medicine shouldn't change your expectations. Stand firm in your beliefs over your child. If you believe he is going to college, then dammit he's going to college, and medicine wont stop him. If you believe she is going to be a prima ballerina, then Misty Copeland move over.

Taking medication for behavior does not have to be a long-term disability, nor does it have to be life or death. Unfortunately, it does become those due to the poor way we approach the situation. Tell the whole truth or say nothing at all. The truth being, yes your child has to take a pill daily to assist with their responsibilities but you still expect them to do great work, be respectful and bring home their coat. (Just kidding, but why do kids leave the coats so often.) The other option is to say nothing at all, meaning crush that shit up, put it in their morning orange juice and before they head inside

> Put it in their orange juice.

the school building let your baby know that you expect them to do great work, be respectful and bring their coat home. It's not lying. They don't need to know, because hopefully they won't be taking it for long anyway.

Medicine allows your child to focus long enough for you to set expectations and teach them strategies for disappointment, disagreement, and whatever other dis words that may cause them to act irrationally. You must equip your children with the necessary coping skills for survival; if not, a lack of medication may lead to their demise. It's a harsh but a true reality. Remember, if we never teach them how to adjust, then we're giving them the act-however-you-want-cause-you-didn't-take-your-medicine card. That card is pulled out a lot when you're small. Really, it's like *VISA* to toddlers, and elementary-aged kids, accepted everywhere. It saddens me too; because those are the ages we should be pushing coping strategies and talking them through their feelings. The card becomes more selective in middle school, like *American Express*. Only a few people like close relatives, parents, grandparents, and certain teachers will take it. Nobody else will deal with the card. Your child will start getting kicked out of classes, you'll begin to notice that your sister only visits when your child is gone, their school friends have only come to visit once, and never returned. Stuff like that. Then, starting around the age of 17, after the voice changes, the height plateaus and the body matures, they reach *AMEX Black* status. Aw shit! Now, the only people who allow your child to swipe the crazy card is Mom, Dad, and the Grands'. Nobody else gives a flying fuck about their pill and excuse of why they didn't take it. Your kid looks like an adult. Your kid talks like an adult. Your kid is just as strong as any adult. Your kid will get their ass whooped by an adult, if they try any slick shit. And, if an adult feels threatened and mismatched, your kid may be shot by an adult.

I have heard a policeman say, "Stop, hands up." I've heard them say, "License and registration please." But, I have never heard them say, "STOP, Did you remember to take your pill this morning?"

If you are not going to teach strategies or you believe your child will never be able to stop taking medication, make it a priority. If you know your child needs this pill to function daily as a "normal" citizen in the world, taking it should be just as important as brushing their teeth and getting dressed. Hell, it can be considered a part of their outfit. Just like the shirt and pants, that little pill also serves as their armor. It is ludicrous to think of leaving the house without a shirt or pants. It should be just as ludicrous to think of them leaving without the medication you know they need to be successful. Make it important. Make it a part of the morning routine. Wake up, wash up, get dressed, take pill, put on

> Make it a part of the morning routine.

shoes. Wake up, wash up, get dressed, take pill, put on shoes.

What teachers' want is for parents to tell the truth or say nothing at all. Arm your kids with everything they need to be successful; paper, pencil, and the pill. Most importantly, do not let your expectations waver. The children will do it, if you demand that it's done.

CHAPTER 5

Tired of Ignoring the Lack of Priority

So, this actually happened. I had a student. He was a nice kid. He was smart even though he found reading extremely difficult. And at times, so was controlling his anger. I liked him and enjoyed him in my class but he definitely kept me on my toes. In the 180 days it takes to complete one academic year, I am sure that I called his parents more than a few times for his low academic performance or asshole-ish behavior. Each time I called, rather each time they answered, I was pacified. Any time he went into an anger-raged fit of destruction, they were generally able to calm the child over the phone. Normally, they would always promise to further investigate when he got home. Since he rarely had his homework, I figured this was a lie. Face it, if you don't have time to address something that you can predict is coming nightly, I'm pretty certain you won't have time for something you didn't know was coming at all. So, we did this song and dance of me calling home, them pretending to make time to address the issue, the entire year. Then, on May 24th, the unthinkable happened. On May 24th, the 180th day of school, his father actually came, unannounced, to check on his son! So awesome...and at the very least five months too late. I wasn't gonna give him a standing ovation. I'd been calling at least every other month begging for support to help HIS child, and he came on the last damn day of school to introduce himself. And then, to put the icing on this dysfunctional ass cake his first words were "I know I should've been here sooner..." No shit Sherlock. Stevie Fucking Wonder can see that.

You make time to put gas in your car. You make time to scroll *Facebook* and *Instagram*. You make time to distort your face and put flowers on your head on *SnapChat*. You make time to watch your favorite show, after you illegally download it. You must make time for your children. When it seems as if you don't have time for your kids, we don't either. I'm gonna tell you the truth, the parents that we

> You must make time for your children.

know call to check on their children, make midday pop-up visits to the school, sign their child's homework or agenda nightly, notices the missing homework on the one day the copy machine breaks down; that child is treated like gold. Not because that kid is pretty or super smart, but because the parents care and the circle knows it. The circle includes the parent, teacher, and the child. When the circle is tight, the child generally doesn't act a damn fool because they know the teacher is going to tell mama/daddy/dem, mama/daddy/dem don't play, and

> When the circle is tight, it's hard to be foolish.

mama/daddy/dem won't think the teacher is lying. When the circle is tight, it's hard to be foolish, hell it's hard to breathe.

Oh, but when the circle isn't tight! When the circle is as loose as grandpa's house shoes on your kid's feet, there is nothing but room for mischief and mayhem. Just in case you are not sure if you're the cause of this ill-fitting relationship, allow me to help.

- If you don't know the name of your child's teachers, it's you
- If you let your Pre-K or kindergarten student take the school bus alone to school on the very first day, it's you
- If you didn't give the school your new number, it's you
- If you don't know if your child can read on grade level, it's you

- If you send your child to school daily without a book bag; it's you
- If you send your child's teacher to voicemail when they call, "cause they be on that bullshit", it's you
- If you can't name three of your child's school friends, who are not relatives or neighbors, it's you
- If you have never requested a teacher conference, it's you
- If you don't think it's strange that your child never gets a homework, report cards or progress reports, it's you
- If you are satisfied when your child only receiving an attendance award at awards day, it's you

You sorry-ass parents, you must do better. I know you had to work...two jobs...as the only parent...of five kids...and two are special needs...and your car is down...and you have no family. I get it, I promise I do. But just because it's a good excuse, doesn't make it any less of an excuse. Excuses are like assholes, everybody has them. We are talking about your child and your investment in your child's life. You're not kissing the teachers ass, you are making certain that your favorite person(s) in the world will make better decisions and

> Just because it's a good excuse, doesn't make it any less of an excuse.

go further in life and you did. I hope that's every parents dream. I know it's mine.

When you don't invest time for your kid, they don't invest time in themselves. I wish I had a dollar for every time I was about to call a parent of an unruly child, and the child said "They not gon' answer, they busy." And 9 times out of 10, the little terrors would be right. The parents would not answer! When the child doesn't believe that you genuinely care about them, they choose short-term happiness. They might throw something because that feels good when they're frustrated. They might curse the teacher, because some attention feels better than no attention. Either way you slice it, the student generally ends up with the wrong crowd, doing the wrong thing, letting a short-term happiness decision lead them toward long-term time in the state clinker. Look at it as investing the time in them now, so that they don't invest the time in the penitentiary system later.

What teachers' want you to know, parents, is that the circle is nothing without you. You make up at least 55% of the circle. When you show that you are all in, so is your child, and so is their teacher. When you show that you've got other priorities, so does your child, and so does their teacher. The time is now, your circle needs you.

CHAPTER 6

Tired of Rules Being Dismissed

So, this actually happened...January 4 was the first day of the second semester. Second semester is a pivotal point in the academic year. Students take standardized tests, promotion or retention is determined and most importantly summer vacation is now on the countdown. Second semester is also the spark of a new beginning. Students are allowed a second chance to correct poor study habits and improve grades and embrace a new mindset regarding school and their abilities. Second semester is just as important, if not more than first semester. So, back to January 4th. Billy, of course his name is not Billy, I taught in the 2000s. WARNING: You are about to enter one hellified tangent. One thing I've notice about names is that they are trendy. When I first begin teaching, I taught in the years of Q. All of my students were, Quincy, Quintana, Qurtez, just stick a Q on it. My latter years of teaching were the years of the –avious, so my students had names like Arquaious, Kenjavious, and some were just Tavious. My mom was a teacher too. She taught in the years of the combined names. So, if the mothers name was Tia and the fathers name was Paul, the child was named Paultia. She also taught during the years of the random capital letter in the middle of the name like LaMia, the accent mark on the ending letter e, as in Jamè and my personal favorite, the year of the backwards spelling, James= Samaj'. OK, Im back, sorry. So, back to January 4th, Billy walks in the room and is fresh to def! He's wearing his new $200 *Jordans*; we know the price because he told us. He's wearing his new name brand outfit. It's so exclusive I've never heard of the designer. The outfit matches his $200 *Jordan's*. We know the cost because he told us. He's looking flyy with his new haircut. He feeling good because he's looking good and he sits down raises his hands and asks for a damn pencil. I ask him if he left it in his book bag, and he informs me that he didn't bring a book-bag to school. (Super-duper flyyy with no academic materials also occurs after tax refunds.) What the fuck?! He continues to talk, saying his mom told him that he didn't need

> Super-duper flyy with no academic materials also occurs after tax refunds.

it because we probably weren't going to do much work since it was the first day of school. Allow me to break this down for you. The student brought nothing to write with, nothing to write on, nothing to carry books or work home in, but I'm supposed to look at his cool, flyy ass for eight damn hours, shittin' me.

Without knowing it, these parents have just sent a message to their child and me. And, the message is loud and clear to the both of us...FUCK IT. Fuck school because you don't do anything there. All you need in this life of sin is you and your *Jordans*. (Shout out to Tupac, Jay Z and Beyoncé; whose parents probably named her in the year of the accent mark.) With every action, you must think, what message am I really sending? Your children are always watching... always. They see everything you do, especially when you think they are not watching. They hear everything you say, especially when you think they are not listening. And, they will repeat what you say to their teacher, even when you tell them not to say a word. Whether explicit or inferred, you are always sending a message to your child. Here's another example...

A student came to school on the very first day, with all the requested school supplies, an excitement for learning and a smile that could light the world. What was the problem? ...no uniform. The students parent told them that they would start wearing their uniform in a few weeks after they had wore all of the nice summer clothes they owned.

We have to be conscience of the true message we are sending. We can't dismiss rules just because they don't seem to matter to us. What I have learned from my experience in the classroom is that all rules exist for a reason. Let's take uniforms for instance. Uniforms were put in place to decrease bullying and disguise the economically disenfranchised. I honestly think we have it wrong. Generally, schools have uniforms in elementary and middle school and they dress freely in high school. I know my high school self would be completely disgusted but I truly believe high school students are the ones who need uniforms the most because bullying motivates those students into action. High-school students actually will do whatever it takes to be fashionable. But, because I was an inner-city high school student, I also know that there is no way around it. Even if students have to wear black and white from the *French Toast* uniform catalog, someone will still pair it with a pair of *Gucci* loafers, a *Burberry* blazer or *Cartier* eyewear and the battle continues. After my daughter was born I shopped around for daycare and pre-Kindergarten programs for her. I found it laughable that they all had a uniform. I have never heard a two-year old talk about another two-year olds cheap shirt at snack time, but that's just me. Even though I don't understand the rule, we adhere to

> We can't dismiss rules just because they don't seem to matter to us.

it because we need her to understand the importance of following rules.

What teachers' want from you, parents, is to watch the messages being sent to our children. These are the very same messages they carry with them throughout life. We have to guide them toward greatness. Be prepared is not a rule to teach them to respond with a middle finger. Success is only achieved when preparation meets opportunity. It's an essential lesson of the Boy Scouts and the Girl Scouts for a reason. Preparation makes you a player in this game of life. Dismiss the rules that make no sense to you, is not a rule to teach them. Following the rules is how you save your own life and puts you in the position to create your own path.

CHAPTER 7

Tired of Sensitive Ass Folk

So, this actually happened. I was teaching middle school math, which is amazing within it self, but I was. My students were assigned a math practice sheet. As they asked questions and completed the assignment, I sat with each of them to conference about their work. As I worked with one student, another student claimed to be finished. I quickly, glanced over their work. I told the student, "I can see that number 4 is wrong." I went back to the student I was helping, to allow the other student to correct number 4 and review the rest of her work. I looked up just in time to see her storm out of the door. I continued working with my student. I figured, she would return once she processed her feelings or I called for backup, whichever came first. Well, when she returned, she wasn't alone. I quickly learned that she stormed out and went straight to the guidance counselor. The counselor thought it would be best to speak with me. I was signaled into the hall by the guidance counselor. I instructed my class to continue working, so I could participate in the mini-conference. The guidance counselor spoke, "Mrs. Jackson, you upset Sara when you told her the answer was wrong." Waiting for the punch line, I blatantly stated, "it was." She continued, "Well Mrs. Jackson, we speak to our students with kind words. Instead of telling her it was wrong, try saying I think you should try it again." Confused, I asked, "What's the difference." "She would be able to accept being told to try it again. Also, you hurt her feelings and an apology..." Apparently, I cut my eye so hard she stopped mid-sentence and rephrased, "so she might be a little upset. I just wanted you to know." When I walked back in my room I went to my desk to attempt to process the incident. Sara walked over to my desk. "Counselor Smith said you would apologize for telling me I was wrong." Ladies and gentleman, I was aware that I was the adult in the situation. I was aware that I was a teacher and my contract did not have to be renewed. But, y'all I couldn't do it. I was not apologizing to a twelve year old for some shit that would help HER become a better student and a better person. AND, did this little monster just come to my desk to collect the apology she felt was owed to her. I really couldn't do it. Instead, I said, "I'm not apologizing because your answer was wrong. I will help you get it right. I am sorry for hurting your feelings, that was not my intention." In my mind, that was a compromise I could live with, even though I was irate.

It is our job, parents and teachers alike, to prepare students to be young people in a real world. We are coddling way too much. Can we agree that "try it again", "Look at question 4 one more time", and "I'm not sure about your answer" are all softer ways of saying its WRONG! So why risk stunting educational and personal growth by saying, try it again. The shit is wrong. Does the world care about your feelings, and I'm just the last to know? I don't think you should go around intentionally hurting kids. But, we can't go around sugarcoating everything and think we are preparing them for life beyond school. I wish I could tell a few companies, "You hurt my feelings when you said unfortunately we have chosen another candidate. You should have said apply to this job again." What do you think they would have done or said to me; I'm pretty certain it's along the lines of kick rocks!

Once, I was teaching in a school that had a strong family base. It seemed like everyone was related in some way. It wasn't hard to find a student who had siblings in every grade level. And lets not talk about cousins. There would sometimes be five or six sets of cousins in one grade level. Everybody seemed to be related! Well, one family had a problem with another family. We saw small fires but someone was always there to put them out. One day after a staff meeting, teachers were comparing notes, and we realized that these pesky arguments were occurring more frequently and aggressively. Well, none of us, not one of us were ready for the next morning. When bus 838 pulled up to the school, it was rockin'! Oh, it wasn't a party; it was a massive family brawl. Kids on top of kids, were yelling, fussing, cussing, kicking, and punching. It was crazy. First, all male teachers were called to the bus. They were able to get all of the students off the bus. But then, one "fuck you" from a student, lead to a "come see me then bitch" from another, and the bus fight became a parking lot brawl. Next, all free adults were called for backup. The students were rounded into the office cussing the entire way. These were elementary school students! Once in the office, students were lined up against the perimeter and teachers were spread out like detention officers. The students were still mouthing off to one another but it was ok, because at least they were not fighting... until they were again. One kid pushed the teacher out of the way, ran around him like some double-dribble basketball play and punched another kid in the face. All hell literally broke out again. Administration had to call the police. After some moments of real effort and threats of escorting them to jail, the students calmed down. When the officers went into questioning the root of all the mischief was uncovered.

Apparently, the matriarchs of each family were both dating the same man. When they found out, the man was forced to choose. The woman, who wasn't chosen, had a difficult time accepting the rejection and told her army of kids to fight the other lady's army of kids every time they saw them. Well, when you live in the same neighborhood, attend the same school and ride the same bus, you'll see someone a lot; hence, all of the fighting. How can we expect the kids to appropriately deal with rejection and disappointment, if we can't deal with it as adults?

As long as they live, our kids will experience disappointment and rejection in life. I have not met one person yet who enjoys it, but I also haven't met one person who hasn't experienced it. Isn't it better that they learn how to deal with disappointment in a loving environment, among people who truly want the best for them and can talk them through it? We have to prepare students for the contest

> Isn't it better that they learn how to deal with disappointment in a loving environment?

they won't win, the project that will not receive a perfect score, the academic scholarship they may not receive and the love that won't love them back. We must teach them that at times it's ok to cry, but then you've gotta move right the hell on to the next moment, the next experience, the next disappointment. It's life.

What teachers' want, is for you to not protect your child from life's lessons and their personal growth. We also don't want you to put them in the middle of your fucked up life because you aren't mature enough to deal with your personal disappointments and poor life choices. Allow them to feel hurt and feel pain, but provide a trusted support to offer sound advice toward moving forward.

Tired of the Blame Being Passed

So, this actually happened. A few weeks ago I was watching the news. They were reporting on a classroom fight video that went viral. In the video, two high school boys were pummeling one another. Classroom furniture was pushed around and used as weapons. Students were screaming, running and recording. The two boys stayed pounding and pounding one another. One boy slammed the other headfirst onto the floor. I shivered and squirmed as I watched the video. It was hard to watch. I am a complete chicken shit though. Anyway, after the fight they interviewed a parent of one of the boys fighting. The news anchor asked, "What are your thoughts about todays incident?" I was thinking she would say, I am concerned about the wellbeing of my child, or I am disappointed how the incident escalated, or I am curious about the disciplinary actions that were taken with both students. Nope, this lady had the nerve so say, "I just wanna know where the teacher was during all of this." WHAT?! Then, the anchor asked a student her thoughts, and she said, "the teacher was just sitting there, she could have tried to break it up!"

Those boys were damn near grown and big as hell. What the fuck was a tiny 100-pound female teacher supposed to do for two 200-pound men, throwing 200-pound jabs and tossing 100-pound desks? Exactly, not a damn thing. She made sure the other kids were out of harms way, called for help and waited until it was over. Even if it was a male teacher, you expect him to jump in the fight? Shittin' me! Teachers aren't compensated when they hurt themselves or their possessions during classroom fights. Let my brand new iPhone screen crack while I'm trying to tussle with two hardheads. Sorry isn't going to fix my phone and sorry is all I'll get. Who got time for that? When did everything become the teacher's fault and responsibility? What all do you expect us to do?

> Teachers aren't compensated when they hurt themselves or their possessions during classroom fights.

I remember reading an article on the US News website in February 2016, about a teacher who lost her job after her phone was stolen when she stepped outside of her classroom. The student found nude images on her phone and leaked them on social media. The superintendent stated that it was her fault for leaving students unattended during a four-minute class break and gave her the option of resigning or being fired. Wasn't that nice of him? Now, no teacher is supposed to leave students unsupervised. But, these kids were 16 not 6. The fact that they couldn't control themselves for four minutes at the age of 16 is their parents fault. Now, at 16, you should also have a pretty good understanding of right and wrong; unless, you had amazingly crappy parents, which they may have. At the age

> The fact that they couldn't control themselves for four minutes at the age of 16 is their parents' fault.

of 16 you should also know that stealing is not only wrong but one of the Ten Commandments. Lastly, at 16 you should have been taught to treat people the way you would want to be treated. So intentionally embarrassing your teacher by making her private photo collection available for all to see, should have been decided against sometime before pressing send. BUT instead of blaming the self-absorbed, heartless, hyperactive, thief, the superintendent, students, parents, and society blamed the trusting teacher. The teacher who had no idea what was going on until her vijayjay was spread eagle on iPhones and Androids all across South Carolina and the Continental United States.

Teachers just want to teach the bomb-ass lesson they spent their weekend planning. That's it. Instead we are expected to break up fights we are not in and didn't start, give out our personal cell phone number, spend our lunch time and only pee break helping your child find a working microwave for their noodles, make ourselves available to parents before we clock in and call it a conference, make ourselves available to students after we clock out and call it tutorial, make sure students have all the supplies they need to complete an assignment, like pencils are only sold in August, make sure that all students participate in school activities although they embarrass the school each time we leave the building, not curse back when students call us out of our name, not frisk, break and throw shit when students steal our money, credit cards, keys or phone, not get with parents when they come to our place of employment trying to start some shit, tie shoes, wipe noses, know birthdays, and teach middle names. Newsflash, teachers don't have any magical powers. We have patience and that shit eventually runs thin.

It seems to me that teachers have been taken advantage of for so long, people have actually adopted the extra mile for daily job responsibilities. Our job is to TRY to break up fights but first and foremost, keep the uninvolved students safe. We break

> People have actually adopted the extra mile for daily job responsibilities.

up fights because we care. Our job is to communicate with the parent. We give you our cell phone numbers because we care. Our job is to make sure students receive lunch. We warm up that cold mess you sent because we care. Everyone can tell you the responsibility for the teachers but no one knows their role. It wasn't the teacher's fault those boys were fighting. Just like it wasn't the teacher's fault her phone was stolen. It was the boys, maybe even the parents. They fought because they wanted to fight. They stole because they wanted to steal. Disciplinary actions should have been taken with those boys involved, not the teachers.

What teachers' want is for parents to understand that we are doing our very best. Although we try, our job is not to save the world. Teachers want you, parents, to take responsibility for your part in situations involving your child. Teachers want you, parents, to teach your child to take responsibility in situations involving themselves. Teachers want you, everyone, to know that we are damn tired of being the last-man-on-the-totem-pole-fall-guy. We are tired of every minor misstep leading to unemployment and permanent marks on our teaching certificate. We are tired of being treated as a nonfactor when every American experienced the love and support of a teacher at some point in their life. #TeachersMatter

CHAPTER 9

Tired of Being Taken for Granted

So, this actually happened

-
-
-
-
-
-
-
-
-
-
-
-
-

-
-
-
-
-
-
-
-
-
-
-
-
-
-
-
-
-
-
-
-
-
-
-
-
-
-
-
-
-

NOTHING! Not a damn thing for Christmas, Teacher Appreciation or the Last Day of School gift. Absolutely Nothing. Not even a thank you card. Nothing!

I had a student who was given a project on the solar system to complete by his science teacher. I was a reading, language arts and math teacher at the time. The rule and expectation for each of my students was that choosing not to complete an assignment is never an option. So, fast-forward to the project due date. My students were popping by my room to proudly show their work before submission. I would compliment the projects and tell them how proud I was of their efforts. Now, let me tell you, some projects were awesome, some were crappy but the best work the kid could do without help. Since they tried and tried their best, all students deserved a compliment…. except the one who slowly walked through my door without a project. So, when I asked him the whereabouts of said project, he had the NERVE to tell me, my mama said (file that under phrases I hate), "she didn't want to spend the money because she knows you won't let me not turn one in." I know his mama said it because kids of certain age and comfort level have not developed a BS filter. What I wanted to do was tell him, to go tell his mama, to go fuck herself. What I decided to do, was alter my schedule, ask his science teacher for a one-day extension, sit with him through his lunch period and mine too, to assist him in his research project, go to the store after work to purchase materials for his model, pull him during breakfast the next morning to help him complete his model and walk him to his science class to submit his project and watch his class presentation.

Now that was just my experience with one student. Let's not talk about the endless hugs given to cheer up a rough day, the tissues issued to dry tears, the class parties given to celebrate milestones, the certificates given to acknowledge accomplishments, the packs of oatmeal and cheese crackers purchased just-in-case a student skips a meal, the toys which overflow the treasure box to keep students motivated, the Clorox wipes purchased to clean tables and end the vicious circle of "just a cough", the materials purchased to elevate a lesson, the kind words spoken to build self-esteem, can I stop now? I can go on, and on. What I need you to know is that what a teacher does on a daily basis to build your child up, which is not in our job description, deserves a simple thank you. Just say thank you. Now, don't get me wrong, gifts are nice,

> Just say thank you.

really nice but everyone has different financial circumstances. Everyone can afford a thank you.

Do you know that teachers' salary's suck? Raises are rarely given. Bonuses and overtime are not an option. Very few schools, especially public schools have supply closets. Teachers are expected to purchase the materials needed for their classroom. Yes, teachers are generally given a few reams of paper, pencils and dry-erase markers but it is not nearly enough to meet the expectation for rigorous, hands-on, student-centered, interactive (all that shit is teacher jargon, for fun and involved) lessons for the entire year.

True story, I asked for twelve items at the end of one school year for the start of the next. We generally only get this opportunity once a year, so the materials you request will be your supply for the entire school year. I asked for a two-hole punch, printer, expo dry-erase markers, *Post-it* chart paper, assorted colored markers, assorted colored permanent markers, variety pack of colored copy paper, index cards, dividers, pencils, glue and a clock. A month after school began, I received a repurposed two-hole punch, five glue sticks, 4 expo-dry erase markers, 12 pencils, two reams of white copy paper and one slender container of *Clorox* disinfecting wipes. I said, 12 pencils, for the school year. Hell, I had 14 students on the first day. I guess the plan was for me to assign a pencil for the school year to each student and make four students share, never sharpen the pencils and pray no new students joined our classroom. Instead, I just bought pencils for my classroom.

You'll never know what all a teacher does to support your child's growth and development. Regardless of the one hurtful teacher of your past or the most recent abusive teacher sweeping the inter-webs,

teachers care about your children and want the abso-
lute best for your child. I'm certain the horrible teachers
you've come across did not
start out that way. None of
us do. We join the educa-
tional ranks to make a difference, provide love, insight
and direction, because we're
passionate about educating

> I'm certain the
> horrible teachers
> you've come across
> did not start out
> that way.

young minds. Over time things change. Lately, change
seems to happen within the first five years. Teachers
get tired. They quickly become burnt out from the
overwhelming workload, never meeting state expectations,
spending more of their paycheck on their classroom
than their own educational debt, never feeling appreciated and constantly being undervalued.

What teachers' want is a simple thank you. We
want parents to take a minute to appreciate the love
given to your child on a daily basis. We want you to
give us a high-five, write a note to our principals and
superintendents about our job well done, a box of
chocolates or a gift card...to *Starbucks*. Parents, just
remember to say thanks and teach your kids to do
the same.

CHAPTER 10

Tired of Wasted Time

So, this actually happened. I wish I could say it only happened once, but I can't. I have watched it happen every year over the past ten years, between January and May. It's not bad, it's life, and it's so hard to watch. I'm talking about maturity among 8 year olds.

Most eight year olds in America are in the 3rd grade. At 8 years old, your child is starting to embrace independent problem solving, reading about 90 words a minute, and speaking sentences which include a raised vocabulary. Eight year olds are starting to read for fun, explore and understand numbers and their relationships. Eight year olds also dive into their natural athleticism or creativity. What people don't mention is what I have witnessed over and over again. Eight year olds become solid in their stance on school and life. If the student has always enjoyed school, classwork generally comes easy to them, or they have an amazing support system at home, the students continue to like school. If they hate school, struggle all the way through and feel like they have little to no support, students may decide to tolerate school until the end, but most await the day they can drop out.

A few years ago I saw an old student at the schools holiday program. He was sitting in the audience on a Tuesday at ten o'clock in the morning. I thought it was great that he was there to support his younger siblings. He greeted me with a smile and the only question I could think of was "Why are you not in school?" He smiled, that beautifully perfect smile I remember seeing daily as he walked the halls of elementary school and said, "I don't do that no more." I had no words. He said it so casually, like we were talking about a cigarette habit. As the program went on, I kept hearing his words in my head, "I don't do that no more." He was barely fifteen. Quitting shouldn't be an option, especially when you have no plan for the future. "I don't do that no more." So what do you do? And, more importantly, what did we do? His village, his circle had failed him. I begin to think back to the student he was in elementary. I met him when he was in the third grade. He struggled with reading. He could read, he was just not close to reading on his third grade level. Math came more natural to him, so he generally tried harder and performed better. He didn't have much help at home. He had several younger siblings and since he was just eight I could only imagine how much he had to help instead of receiving help. He always had friends and was pretty mild mannered, unless someone really challenged him. He wasn't scared to fight or be suspended. As I thought back on his life, as I knew it, trying to review the missed red flags from his failed village, the program concluded. I saw him and his mother in the lobby. She looked at me and said, "I know, I know, somebody needs to talk to him!" And I thought to myself, "That's it! That's the failing piece to this puzzle."

You only have until your child is eight to talk. That is only 2,920 days to leave your mark from the day your child is born. Now, they are your kids, so you'll have them for a lifetime. But, if you really want

> 2,920 days to leave your mark.

them to hear you, you must start early. Kids are adorable and everything they do gets one million likes on social media and everyone thinks it's the cutest thing ever. But if it's not cute at 13, it's probably not cute at 3. Think about it, there is always a video going viral of a kid shaking their ass or cussing. Those videos are nothing to share or laugh at, the kid may be cute but their actions are not. You can't post videos of your child talking back at two and be surprised they are telling you to shut the fuck up at thirteen. We must start early.

Some people only use their GPS after they get lost, knowing all along that they have no idea where they are going. Some people use their GPS at the start of the trip, to make sure they get to their destination. As parents, we guide with our words and through our actions. These are our babies, we can't afford to let them get lost in the world and then provide guidance. It is our responsibility to guide them from the start of their journey. Especially since we know that they are going to miss a turn, tune it out, and try it their way along the route. Everyone who uses a GPS does the very same thing. What makes using a GPS wonderful is KNOWING, that you can always refer back to it, if you're in trouble. It's a sense of comfort in having something or someone there in the beginning of your journey. You just kinda know they will be there in the end. The navigational clock starts the moment your child is born.

> There's a sense of comfort in having something or someone with you at the beginning of your journey.

Our children MUST grow up knowing that their parents were always right there, giving them the freedom to go their own way but not without first preparing them with the knowledge necessary for the journey. They must know that you expect them to make a few mistakes, but most importantly you expect them to make it to their destiny. Shit happens, shit always happens, we all know it only takes one wrong turn to go completely off course. Our children must know that after they mess up, you can get them back on the road to greatness.

Teachers' want you to be a GPS for your child, guiding them to their ultimate destinations of college, the workforce or entrepreneurship. Just like the GPS, teachers want you to always be charged, be consistent in your words and actions, and always, always start at the very beginning.

CHAPTER 11

Tired of YOUR Absence

So, this actually happened. I taught a student who was the oldest of three. Each of the siblings attended our school. The students were cute and each had a great sense of humor. The family was mostly remembered for being bad as hell. It was nothing for one of the siblings to be sent to the principal's office, only to find their two other siblings already there. These kids were bad! The eldest had a smart-ass mouth, the middle child had a funky-ass attitude and the youngest was just a bad-ass. I had the joy of having the eldest in my class. This kid would cuss, fuss, fight; he did it all. But, I liked him. He wasn't dumb by anyone's stand-ards. Some would even say he was calculated. One day, I noticed the joy in his face when I threatened to escort him to the principal's office. Before, I could get out my "Don't make me take you..." I noticed his youngest sibling being escorted past our door to the principal's office by his teacher. I decided that I would not feed into what he obviously wanted me to do. I began to ignore his antics and continue with class. The more I ignored, the more wild and obnoxious he became. Then, he kept alluding to being taken to the office. I couldn't figure out why he wanted to get to the office so bad. It was by grace that I didn't snap before I was able to dismiss the class. That kid was trying to push every damn button he could find, and that shit was working too. I asked him to wait after class and he did. Once everyone was gone I asked him, "Why do you want to go to the office so bad?" he look stunned at first, then answered with a shrug and "I don't know." I told him that I didn't believe him and I was certain he knew why. Remember, this kid was smart. He was very much in control of his actions. For some reason, that was enough for him to open up. He told me, "Every time I get sent to the office, they call my dad. He doesn't live with us anymore and I miss him. I only get to see my dad when the school calls him" So, we made a deal that day. I would allow him to call his dad from my phone and I would give his dad a good report, each day he behaved and completed his assignments.

Generally, we teachers are placed in the middle of your shit. We have students yell at us, cuss at us, attack us, for reasons that rarely have anything to do with us. The children are yelling for their parent's attention. The children are cursing to get their parent's attention. They want you, not us.

I understand the way it starts, kids cost money. I damn near fell to the floor when I opened the bill for mine after her birth and I had insurance. To make matters worse, that's just the first bill; they need things, education and recreation. The bills associated with your child alone can blow your mind. So you begin to work harder for them, to provide the necessities and a few extra things they want which makes life more enjoyable. Then, one late night at the office leads to fifty, and you can't remember the last time you tucked your child into bed. You can't remember the last time you played their favorite board game. You can't remember the last time you laughed together. You can't remember the last time you said, "Good job kid!" and sealed it with a hug or high-five.

Teachers will tell you that the power of a hug and a high-five are mighty! You can get kids to do some of everything with the promise of simple hug or high-five. Everyone likes to feel good. Everyone wants to feel loved and appreciated. Think about it, you go to work for your check, but when your boss

> Everyone likes to feel good.

acknowledges your efforts, you beam with pride. You relish that new temporary parking spot, you polish your new plaque, and you even treasure your new certificate. Kids feel the exact same way. They don't get a check, but most can bank on praise from the teacher. That makes you parents, the big boss. When you acknowledge their efforts, support their ideas and encourage them to strive for more, there is nothing anyone can say to top that. The best part is the cost of kind words, a hug and a high-five are all free! It will cost you absolutely nothing; but your time. You must make the time.

What teachers' want parents… is for you to be there.

CHAPTER 12

Tired of Being Tired

10 Things I Think Every Parent Should Know

1. Reality shows are not for kids. Please tell your children reality shows are shows. That shit is not real life. When is the last time you went to lunch with a bunch of bitches you can't stand. These kids are in school fighting and acting a damn fool because they think this is how life goes. Stop letting TV raise your kids and talk to them. They shouldn't be watching that mess anyway.

2. There is such a thing as a dumb question. Quit telling your kid that it isn't. The question asked, that was just answered a second before is dumb. Asking the date when it's written on the board, next to the calendar on the wall, is dumb.

3. I tried is not something you say because you have lips that move and a voice. Trying takes effort. Please let your child know that when they finish a test before the teacher is done passing it out, that's not trying. That's that bullshit. Trying is when you make an EFFORT to do something. Shading C all the way down the bubble sheet shows that your child is trying to get an F.

4. Ain't nobody lying on your child. We've got other things to do than sit home and concoct elaborate lies about your child stealing a pencil or smacking another kid in the head. They did the shit, deal with it.

5. Bedtimes are not just for babies. Bedtime is for <u>your</u> baby. If your kid is in elementary or middle school, their asses should be in bed before primetime TV begins. You wanna know why they aren't tired by primetime TV's start, because they slept all through math class.

6. Tell children to think for themselves. Repeating after the loud kid is going to get them in trouble every time. Everyone knows the loudest student is the wrongest student. Now, people think your kid is dumb too.

7. TV and computer time aren't necessary every night, dinner is. TV and computer time should be earned, **at least regulated**. If I have one more eight-year-old try to tell me about a World Star Hip Hop video they saw, I'm going to scream. That shit is not for kids.

8. Read to your child. Start reading to them at conception. They can hear you. Read to them as newborns and as infants. Although, you cannot understand their language, they are learning yours. Speak to them using real words. Continue to <u>read to them each night</u> as toddlers and preschoolers. The books help build their vocabulary and a love for reading. Go to the bookstore on the weekend. It is the best free activity! You can read all the good books, and then go home. As your child continues to grow, they will learn the types of books they enjoy reading. Don't wait for your child to pick up a book to begin reading to them. Definitely don't wait until they start school, you're setting them up to be the slowest and lowest reader in the class. Struggle ain't fun.

9. EVERYTHING IS NOT BULLYING! I have come to loathe this word. Sometimes your child is a complete nuisance. If the big kid repeatedly asked your precious baby to stop singing during the test because he couldn't concentrate, and your baby responded with, "make me, it's a free world and I can sing as much as I want because I'm not hurting anyone." That punch your child received was the result of a challenged accepted.

10. Although, teachers like to think it, we are not geniuses. We did not make up multiplication or verb-tense. Most of us Googled it and you can too. Quit sending back work saying you didn't

understand. The three words you need to know are lesson, practice and video. If you need to know how to help your child with multiplication, search multiplication lesson. If your child isn't quite getting it and needs extra help, search multiplication practice. If you and your child are more visual or they want tablet time during the week, search multiplication video. Stop asking for extra shit and making excuses about why something wasn't done. Now, you too have the power. You're Welcome.

Refresher

I started teaching to fight the war on educational equality. After a while, I realized that I had been fighting for years nonstop and I could see no real positive change. I didn't even know who I was fighting; it became more blurred each year. Am I fighting the system? Am I fighting administration? Am I fighting the parents? Am I fighting the students? Am I fighting myself? The truth is, I still don't know. What I do know is this is not a fight I am willing to stop fighting. I have just decided to fight my way, with my words. It is my hope that this book breaks down the parent teacher walls of communication. It is my hope that this book ignites conversations among the village that were not previously had. It is my hope that this book helps one caring parent that just needs a friendly reminder of who's really important in their life. It is my hope that this book unites parents and teachers to fight this war on educational equality together. Our children need us. Let's fight for them.

Educationally Yours,

Traci D. W. Jackson

A portion of the proceeds will be donated to Yellow Bus Education, Inc. Yellow Bus Education, Inc. is an educational non-profit organization which use field trip experiences to teach educational standards to school-aged youth. More information about Yellow Bus Education can be found at www.yellowbused.org.

Made in the USA
Lexington, KY
30 May 2017